L504

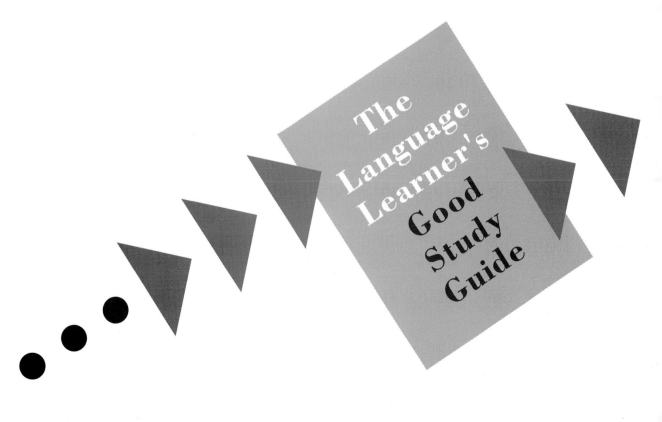

The Language Learner's Good Study Guide

L504 course team

Core course team

Anne Stevens (course team chair)
Lore Arthur
Stephen Hagen
Stella Hurd
Bernard Kavanagh
Marie-Noëlle Lamy
Monica Shelley
Duncan Sidwell
Gail Barron (course manager)
Jo McDonald (course manager)
Kate Laughton (editor)
Ann Breeds (secretary)
Christine Sadler (secretary)

Consultant author

Sandra Truscott

Course production team

Jonathan Davies (design co-ordinator)
Tony Duggan (project control)
Pam Higgins (designer)

External assessor

Professor James Coleman (University of Portsmouth)

Cartoons by Gary Rees

The Open University, Walton Hall, Milton Keynes MK7 6AA

First published 1995. Reprinted 1996, 1997, 1998

Edited, designed and typeset by The Open University

Printed in the United Kingdom by Henry Ling Ltd, Dorchester DT1 1HD

ISBN 0 7492 6297 4

If you would like a copy of *Studying with the Open University* or more information on Open University language materials, please write to the Course Enquiries Data Service, P.O. Box 625, Dane Road, Milton Keynes MK1 1TY.

1.4

L504booki1.4

Contents

1 Introduction

As you open this guide to learning a language, millions of people all over the world are already involved in second-language learning. In China, hundreds of thousands of people have completed the phenomenally successful English language course *Follow Me*. In the Canadian province of Quebec, native English speakers know they need to learn French if they are to take a full part in the cultural and civic life of their province. Many millions of North Americans learn Spanish, in a country where the number of native Spanish speakers is fast approaching that of English speakers, especially in the southern states.

There are many reasons for learning a language. Perhaps you only want to speak the language so that you can communicate with friends or colleagues, or you may be prompted by a wish to read original texts in the language or to watch foreign films or television programmes. Your reason will determine what, for you, is the most important and useful part of your learning.

You will always find that more knowledge and information is presented to you than you can possibly remember. Be selective about what you learn, but be guided by any study notes and hints for learning that are provided in your course materials. By building your own body of language, you will discover the pleasures of language learning and you will almost certainly find many ways of applying your new knowledge and skills.

You may have passed an 'O' level some years ago or picked up some language on your holidays. You may feel that you're rather 'rusty' or that you're not too sure about some of the basics. Don't let this worry you. Learning a language is not an easy process and it takes time. Some parts, like the vocabulary, have to be memorized and others, such as pronunciation and intonation, need practice. You will certainly need to get plenty of practice in the four skills – reading, writing, speaking and listening – to enable you to consolidate and develop your expertise. You will find some things easier than others. Try to become aware of **how** you learn and alert to what, for you, is easier or more difficult. As you work through your course materials, record how you learned as well as what you achieved. You will soon recognize your own strengths and weaknesses and discover which learning strategies you find most helpful.

In this guide we deal with some of the practicalities (and theoretical issues) of learning a modern foreign language. Some of the ideas relate to studying in general and are concerned with memory, organization and learning theory. You may be familiar with them already. If not, and you want to find out more about this area, it's worth reading *The Good Study Guide* (Northedge, A., 1991, The Open University, ISBN 0 7492 0044 8). Other ideas will be quite new to you, especially if you're coming back to language learning after a long time.

There are ways of making the long-term goal of learning a language pleasurable and less time-consuming. Everyone can be a language learner, whatever their age, background or learning experience. This guide has been written to introduce you to a number of different ways of learning and to encourage you to explore and develop your own learning style. Every foreign-language learner is an individual, starting from a different point, with different levels of aptitude and interest. We hope to introduce you to a range of strategies which you can adapt to suit your needs. You don't need to adopt them all: some you may feel are unhelpful, unnecessary or even silly. Choose those that suit you – but make sure you put them into practice.

Before reading any further in the guide, we suggest that you buy a large A4 file or ring-binder, which you will use to build up a dossier of your own materials. It doesn't matter which course book or language programme you're studying – the aim here is to 'personalize' your dossier and make it a really useful resource for you. You could start off with a page called 'Hints and advice for study' where you note down the advice on language learning in this guide that you find useful and write in the results of the activities we ask you to complete as you work through the guide. Once you start on your language-learning course, you can note down grammar points or new vocabulary items as they crop up. How you organize the dossier is up to you, but you'll probably find it helpful to have separate sections for these and for other main areas such as listening, reading, writing and speaking skills and for cultural notes. If you're using a ring-binder for your dossier, divider cards would be useful. You may prefer to use a set of files or to store information on a personal computer.

Two fundamental principles of language learning have emerged from this introduction: first, that it is a very personal thing; second, that it has to be active. You need to keep these two principles in mind as you work through your chosen language course.

There is a lot of material to be absorbed in this guide and you will find that much of it will make more sense once you have started to study. Use the guide as you would a reference manual, referring to it as you progress through your foreign-language course.

2 How to learn a language

In this section we talk first about learning in general and then about language learning in particular. You'll be asked to complete several practical activities to encourage you to reflect on what you're reading.

The more you know about how to learn, the more efficiently you are likely to work and the more benefit you will obtain from your studies. Most of us lead busy lives and we need to use the few spare hours that we do have as effectively as possible. You are also encouraged to start thinking about how **you** like to learn, that is, your preferred learning style, how to build on your strengths and how to minimize any weaknesses.

Motivation

The more motivated you are to learn, the more likely you are to succeed. It may seem an obvious point, but knowing why you want to learn – and, more importantly, sustaining your level of motivation – is crucial to your success.

One of the best ways of maintaining your enthusiasm and morale is to find a study partner: this could be someone in your own family or a friend with a similar level in the foreign language that you're learning. Since language learning is about communication, working with another person makes sense on a practical level as well.

ACTION POINT

Think of someone you could work with on a regular basis – a colleague, friend or relative perhaps. Agree to keep in touch to sort out problems and to practise the language.

Many adults feel that they're too old to study effectively: they complain about failing memories or the inability to get their tongue round awkward sounds in a foreign language. However, adult learners tend to have a high level of motivation, good self-discipline and an appreciation of learning strategies. These are major advantages in the efficient learning of a language.

But even adults have their moments of disillusionment and disappointment when they feel they're making little progress and are tempted to admit defeat. To help to motivate you afresh, try the following activity. Pin up the results where you can read them if you need to or put them in the 'Hints and advice for study' section in your dossier.

ACTION
POINT Think about how you will benefit in the long run from being able to read and speak another language. List as many reasons as you can think of. Here are some suggestions to start with.

- I'll be able to see that new foreign film and understand a lot without the help of subtitles.

- I'll be able to avoid the difficulties I had last year when I tried to change some traveller's cheques.

- I'll be able to avoid the embarrassment I felt in Marbella when I was taken ill and could not explain what was wrong.

- If my car breaks down when I'm driving on the continent, a mechanic will be able to understand me.

- I'll be able to socialize with the nice French people we met at the campsite in Brittany.

- I'll be able to avoid the embarassing situation I faced last year when Herr Hofmeyer took me out to dinner on the marketing trip and I couldn't take part in the general conversation.

Autonomous learning

Autonomous learning means learning on your own. Here are some of the implications of self-study or home learning.

Taking responsibility for your own learning is important at all stages in the educational process – which is why self-study and flexible learning programmes are increasingly seen as important at all levels of education. It is even more important if you're learning on your own or attending a weekly evening class.

So what does autonomy mean in practical terms? It's helpful to think about this in stages:

- defining your objectives;
- prioritizing your objectives;
- planning your study routine.

Defining your objectives

Think about the list you made of your reasons for learning a language. If these reasons are rather vague, tighten them up into more specific objectives. For example, what was originally 'improving my French/German/Italian/Spanish' might become something like 'I aim to be able to read some of the news in the foreign press by the end of the month'.

Here are some other suggestions to help you sharpen up your objectives.

- Introduce a deadline so that you know how fast (or slowly) you need to reach a particular goal.

- Put a list of your objectives somewhere where you will see it (on the back cover of your dossier perhaps) and review it frequently. This will help keep you on target.

- You may decide that you need to adapt your objectives. You may have been too hard (or too easy) on yourself. If you feel that you can go beyond what turns out to be a modest objective, increase it. If, on the other hand, you have taken on too much, modify your objectives. There is no failure in this. You are simply being realistic about what is and is not possible.

Besides long-term objectives, you'll need to set yourself short-term goals, within a particular timescale. These might be achievable on a daily or weekly basis. For example, your weekly goal might be to complete a set amount of work from your course book. Your daily goal might be to memorize ten new words or to learn by heart the vocabulary you have worked on that day. List these goals and, again, place them where you will see them frequently. Tick them off as you complete them. This will give you a sense of achievement.

Prioritizing your objectives

You also need to prioritize your objectives. There may be times when you can't achieve what you set out to do. Sort out which items on your list are the most important and make sure that these are completed first. If you miss out or forget to do any, carry them over to the next day. But be honest about prioritizing.

You might find that there are certain things which always get left to one side. It is a good idea to set aside time for completing the items which never seem to get to the top of the list. This might be first thing in the morning, for instance, when you feel at your best for tackling off-putting jobs such as learning difficult vocabulary.

Planning your study routine

You need to decide which times of the day suit you best for study. They will, of course, be competing with all the other claims on your time. If you are in full-time employment, you may decide to use your lunch break to study. Again, unless you are a night owl, our advice is the earlier the better. You can then relax, knowing that you've already finished your study for the day. Early in the day is also when you're likely to be less tired and more receptive.

Organizing your study time

You cannot plan and prioritize your objectives without apportioning your time. One sensible solution might be to set aside half an hour or an hour a day for language study. On some days you might want to do more in order to give a more intense period of time to your study. Or perhaps you would rather devote the whole of Sunday to study and get the week's work out of the way in one go. This is the sort of pattern that many of us followed earlier in our education, especially when preparing for exams. But sometimes this model is not such a good idea. Language needs regular and constant practice. Little and often – the regular time each day technique – is a better option for a number of reasons.

- Because we are talking about acquiring a skill (like playing the piano) rather than absorbing a body of information, it makes sense to take a more gradual approach.
- This approach is less daunting and, if properly managed, much easier to achieve. It is also much less tiring.
- It builds in time for reviewing earlier material.
- Repeated exposure to the language will help you to remember material more easily.
- It takes time for vocabulary and new structures to take root and be transferred from short- to long-term memory.

'Prime' versus 'low-grade' time

Something else to consider is the quality of your time and what sort of study you'll be doing when. The half an hour/hour a day model is 'prime time' – that is, time when you're feeling relaxed and alert and know that you're not going to be interrupted. This is when you should read your materials and complete written and oral tasks. If you decide to have a longer study session, you can improve your absorption of new information by taking frequent breaks. Have a cup of coffee in your break or post a letter. A short burst of physical activity often stimulates concentration.

'Prime time' – time when you're feeling relaxed and alert and know that you're not going to be interrupted.

You will also have 'low-grade' time available: perhaps when you're travelling to work or washing up or when you may be interrupted. This time can be used very profitably in listening again to recorded material or practising out loud an exercise you worked on the day before.

ACTION POINT

Think about what 'low-grade' time you have available and the sort of activities that you could do then. We've started off the list with some ideas.

- If you have a personal stereo, use it to listen to your language cassettes while you're waiting for a bus or train or out jogging.

- Tune into a foreign radio station. Even if you don't understand very much at first, you'll be attuning yourself to intonation (the rise and fall of the voice in phrases and sentences) and to pronunciation in general.

- If you have cable or satellite TV, you may be able to receive foreign television. If you're thinking of investing in a system, consider paying a little extra for one which receives a wider range of satellites. TV5 Europe is an excellent channel if you wish to listen to French. TVE (Televisión Española) is good for Spanish learners, as is the Hispasat satellite, which broadcasts four different Spanish language channels. You can also listen to audio channels via satellite: they give a much better reception than radio.

- Look in the newspapers for schools broadcasts in foreign languages. Many of these programmes appeal to adults too.

- If you have a computer, you'll find lots of routine language activities are quite fun. You may be able to buy a spell checker in your chosen foreign language or you might consider obtaining a foreign-language version of your word-processing package.

Making yourself comfortable

It is a good idea to keep your equipment (books, dossier, dictionary, audio and video tapes and cassette player) at hand, ready for when you want to study. If your materials are accessible, you are more likely to use odd moments for looking up a grammar point, reading a text or learning some vocabulary. You might find that music is a good background for study. Some modern methods of language learning deliberately use certain kinds of classical music to promote the relaxed state which allows the brain to absorb new material more readily. It is also thought that listening to or reading the foreign language immediately before going to sleep encourages the mind to work through this material, in much the same way as dreams work through recent events or anxieties in your life. These ideas are controversial, but you lose nothing by trying them out and discovering if they work for you.

Taking risks and learning from mistakes

Attitudes to mistakes have changed radically in the theory and practice of language learning. In fact, without the freedom to make and learn from mistakes, there can be no improvement or progress.

Sticking to what you know is right may have made for good exam marks at school and may make you feel 'safer', but it is very restrictive and limits your learning. Instead of moving on to a higher level of performance, you remain on a plateau. Good language learners take risks. They will sometimes get into linguistic trouble, but it is rarely fatal and almost always results in learning.

You can use mistakes diagnostically to assess which language areas you have understood and internalized and which ones will need further practice and time. For example, after completing a written exercise in your course book or a spoken activity on cassette, go back and check it carefully to see where you went wrong, and why. Most modern language courses have a key to help you check your answers. The ones you get wrong may be as important as those you get right. Your mistakes may tell you that you need to review a particular grammatical point or to revise some tricky spellings before continuing to the next set of exercises. Note any corrections and explanations in your dossier and read them over in the following few days to make sure you've understood and remembered.

It is important to remember that in mother-tongue language learning children make grammatical errors at various points in their development. There is thought to be some sort of order in which structures are acquired, and this order does not always follow what seems to be the most logical progression. It is not certain whether this is true in second-language learning, but if it is, then it would mean that making mistakes is not only normal but inevitable and necessary at key stages in our linguistic development.

ACTION POINT

Think of any occasions when you made an error in a foreign language, or even in English. How did you ensure that it did not happen again?

Remember that what you are doing and saying as you study your foreign-language materials is only a rehearsal for a future performance. In rehearsal you have the right to play and experiment with the language. Take every advantage of that position.

Devising useful and practical activities

If this is not your first attempt at learning a language, you may feel that previous efforts were unfruitful and that you are not a 'successful' language learner. This may be due to a number of factors: the teaching style, the course book, a lack of relevance in the content. The key to language learning is to ensure that what you learn is relevant and useful to you. The more you personalize your work, the more proficient you will become.

Making language relevant

There may be times when you wonder why you are being asked to do a certain activity or moments when you think that a particular exercise or topic is uninteresting or irrelevant. While most course materials are carefully designed with a particular purpose in mind, there will always be some areas which you find more interesting than others.

Always try to make every activity as relevant and meaningful to you as possible, so that you can derive the maximum benefit and pleasure from it. To give an example: you may know that you are shaky on the past tenses of certain verbs and that you need to review them. Why not put each of these verbs into a sentence which expresses something personal and which you may wish to say on a future occasion? This has several advantages.

- You are more likely to remember the form if it is contained within a sentence.

- You are more likely to remember the sentence if it says something personal to you.

- You will already have rehearsed language that you mean to use in the future.

You can also adapt ideas for your own purposes. For instance, if you're introduced to a short dialogue which practises some specific language points, you could invent your own dialogue which contains the same learning points but which refers to something that has happened to you.

ACTION POINT

Create a section in your dossier which is devoted to a personal study plan and start to make a list of ideas about how you could transform the course material into examples and tasks that relate to your interests and needs. You may not be able to think of many ideas at this stage, but more will occur to you as you work through the material. Add them to your list.

Being active

It also helps if you are positively and physically involved in the learning process. This involvement can take many forms. Here are a few ideas.

- As a matter of routine, always speak the material out loud in the foreign language, whether you are asked to do so or not.

- You could take this one step further and record yourself speaking, then listen to yourself critically, playing back what you have recorded the next day, perhaps on your car cassette player if you drive to work.

As a matter of routine, always speak the material out loud ...

- You could set up a filing system in which all new vocabulary items are noted on dossier pages or index cards. Next day, when you have a moment or two, look through the cards to remind yourself of the spelling, gender and meaning of the new vocabulary. It is a good idea to jot down key points in a small pocket notebook and carry this around with you so that you can look at it from time to time.

You'll probably be able to think of lots more activities which will ensure that you are thinking about, and consequently absorbing, new information. Here are a few suggestions about how you might organize a study session.

Whenever you finish reading a text in the foreign language, listening to an audio extract or watching a video sequence, go through the following procedure if you have time before doing any exercises set for you in your course book.

- Write down immediately all the words and phrases you can remember from what you have just heard or read. It does not matter what order they are in; just note them down as they come into your mind. Write them in a column on the left-hand side of a piece of paper. There may be some ideas that come back to you in English rather than in the foreign language. This might happen if you are working with video where the image helps you to remember the idea rather than the language.

- Listen/watch/read again and then:
    - correct the words/phrases if you did not get them quite right;
    - write down the foreign-language equivalent of any words/phrases which you noted in English.

At this stage, don't worry about all the language you've forgotten or not understood (this may well be explained in your course book), but do look up anything you particularly want to know. In doing this, you will pinpoint those areas that you have not understood or have not heard properly and you can pay particular attention to them later on. Whenever you hear new sounds, try to work out how they are spelled. Whenever you see new words in print, work out how they will sound.

If you do not have time for that, try to do the following.

- Having read/watched/listened, sit back, close your eyes and try to recall as much as possible of what you've just read/watched/listened to.

- Read or listen or watch again and then repeat the recall process described above before starting work on any exercises which have been set.

- At the end of your study session, sit quietly for a few minutes and go through everything in your head again. Start by trying to remember the material on the audio and video cassettes, the lists you made, the exercises you completed – in fact all the work you did.

- If you have time, listen to or watch the audio and video material again and this time try to remember the words around the ones you put in your list.

Don't try to learn things by heart if this strategy does not appeal to you. Just try to recall and let things come into your mind. You won't remember everything, but what you have to do is to give yourself plenty of varied opportunities to improve your memory processes.

In between study sessions, go over in your mind what you have learned. You can do this on the bus, while doing the washing up or when you take the dog for its evening stroll. Gradually, without too much forcing, try to recall the written texts, the video and audio material, the lists you've compiled and the exercises you've completed. The more time you spend trying to remember actively, the less language you'll forget.

Watch/listen to video and audio material again and again, whenever you can. This private work of your own is at least as important as doing the exercises and written work in your course book. You can make good use of the transcripts of the material where they are given. You will find these transcripts helpful when revising language or checking spellings. You can also improve your pronunciation by listening or viewing with the transcript. This provides a useful link between the written and spoken language.

Using a multi-sensory approach

Finally, as you learn, try to engage as many senses as you can. The more ways you can experience the language – through hearing, seeing, reading and repeating out loud – the better are your chances of retaining it. If you are someone who can learn easily – perhaps you have only to see a word written on a list to remember it – fine. Remember, though, that good language learners use a variety of skills – memory, mimicry, seeking and perceiving patterns, and so on – and acquiring these skills calls for a variety of approaches.

In his novel *À la recherche du temps perdu* Marcel Proust describes how, upon eating a *madeleine,* or small cake, dipped in tea, his long-forgotten childhood memories and emotions came flooding back. The sense of taste was so powerful that it triggered memories which had long since been locked away. You may have the same sensitivity towards colour or scent, which you can use to associate with words or facts. For example, some language learners note down new vocabulary items in different coloured inks to denote gender. They think that colour can help them remember masculine, feminine or neuter words. If you're using your dossier for noting vocabulary, you could try setting out new words and phrases in this way to see if you find it helpful. A language-learning approach called TPR (Total Physical Response) associates movement with language. Students learning commands like 'shut the door' or 'open the window' physically carry out these actions as they say the words; they are learning by doing. From time to time, you could try using the foreign language to describe what you're doing. If your course materials do not provide you with examples of simple poems or songs, why not go along to your local library and borrow a poetry book or cassette? Singing along to music or reading a poem out loud can heighten your sense of sound, rhyme and rhythm. This in turn should improve your intonation and your pronunciation of the foreign language.

Marcel Proust's brain being triggered

Self-evaluation

Whether or not you attend a regular class or group, you will want to know how you are progressing. Self-evaluation, that is assessing your own progress, can be carried out in simple ways by making use of elements within the course materials. Some self-evaluation is relatively straightforward because it is based on written exercises. Most modern language courses have a key at the back of the course book or an 'Answers' supplement so that you can check your work.

It is often possible to re-work an exercise by taking the key or model answer as your starting point. If you do this some time after first completing the exercise, you will be able to judge how much of the work you have really assimilated and how much you have forgotten in the intervening period. There are many other areas, for example speaking skills such as fluency and pronunciation, where re-working earlier tasks and exercises helps to improve your level of skill and gives you an observable difference in performance.

Recording your progress

So how do you carry out such self-evaluation? One good idea is to mark each written exercise you do and keep a record of these marks. This not only helps you become aware of your progress, but will remind you later of where you need to do more practice. You should also record how long the work took, as progress includes working faster as well as more accurately. Note, too, your strengths and weaknesses in particular areas of language or types of exercise. You could start a new section in your dossier, entitled 'Self-evaluation' or 'Progress', and keep this record or diary there.

- Your records should include notes on specific grammatical errors or suggested improvements in the use of vocabulary, and the strategies you have used to eradicate these errors and incorporate improvements. You could divide mistakes under headings such as:

    - spelling;

    - tenses;

    - gender;

    - word order.

- You can also include global comments on your competence in various areas: here you could mention problems with pronunciation in general and with certain sounds in particular.

- You should also record your thoughts on the learning techniques that work best for you.

Reflecting on your learning

As you progress through the language material you are studying, you will become more aware of how you learn best and what type of work appeals to you. True progress involves working not only on these appealing parts of the language, but also on those aspects which you find difficult. Make regular checks on your record of progress to remind yourself of what has worked well for you. If you find speaking difficult, try practising when you are on your own.

You should then see an improvement and feel less inhibited when you have to use the language more publicly.

Which techniques work best for you? Do you need to see everything written down? Does the written word interfere with pronunciation?

After each study session make a few notes on the content of your language learning and on the way you tackled the session, how you tested yourself and which areas you need to improve, particularly if you require a lot of practice when something goes wrong. All this will stand you in good stead in the future.

If you are conscientious about keeping your records up to date, you will find that by the end of the course you will have a personal profile of your achievements. This will enable you to see how well you have progressed over a long period and to decide which areas you need to work on in order to reach the objectives you have set yourself.

ACTION POINT

Think about how you are going to set out the results of your self-evaluation. Set aside one page in your dossier for each chapter, section or unit of your course materials or course book. Give yourself plenty of space for filling in:

- the mark you award yourself for each activity, with your reasons for that particular assessment;
- a general comment on your performance.

3 Thinking about language patterns

The place of grammar in language courses is quite controversial. Many adults like to start with grammar rules because they help them learn; others prefer to listen or read first and then to work out the grammar for themselves. In this section we provide an overview of what grammar is and discuss what other systems help to organize language.

Some people associate grammar with rote learning and drills; others remember it fondly as supplying the rules underlying the structure of a language. Much depends on whether you prefer to learn the structure first and then attack the other elements of the language, or vice versa.

It may take some of the fear out of grammar if you think of it simply as a skeleton on which language hangs: it does not exist independently, but is just one aspect of speech and language. The bare bones of grammar are few and easily learned. Much more effort has to be put into fleshing out the skeleton with all the other elements that make up the organism.

Acquisition and learning

People who find it easy to learn languages follow rules which are acquired unconsciously, as they go along. You may be one of the lucky ones who can learn in this way and has the opportunity to do so. This way of learning is sometimes called 'acquisition' or 'natural learning' and takes place through being exposed to a language. Native speakers, for example, start learning this way from birth. Some learners of foreign languages need to hear only a limited amount of the language to be able to pick it up quickly. Many adult learners, however, need the structure to be systematically explained, for example through a course of instruction.

This is where grammar comes in. It provides a short cut to learning, because it enables us to see patterns instead of individual phenomena. Through the study of grammar, we can systematize and therefore speed up the learning process. Grammar also provides the vocabulary for describing the role that words play in sentences. It is useful to know what function adverbs, adjectives or prepositions perform in sentences and how they combine to make the language meaningful.

- Knowledge of grammar helps us talk about the language as well as use the language and thus speeds up the learning process.
- Grammar works as shorthand to avoid clumsy constructions like 'a doing word' (or verb) or a 'describing word' (or adjective).
- It helps us use a dictionary more effectively.

But learning grammar is not an end in itself: knowing the whole of the grammar of any language is not going to make us speak perfectly or listen effectively. Only practice can do that.

Making generalizations

If grammar is to be learned, it doesn't follow that you have to start with the rules in grammar books. There is another, much more interesting way that places more of the onus on you, the learner, to become actively involved in making your own generalizations about grammatical points.

Suppose a non-English speaker wants to learn how to describe films in English, particularly to enthuse about a film which she/he considers to be really good. A lot can be learned from flicking through a 'What's on' type magazine or listing. A glance at one yields the following comments on a film:

> A great performance.
>
> One of Ivory's greatest films.
>
> A fine portrayal of artistic anguish.
>
> The finest film of the year.

From this, learners could make two generalizations. First, in English adjectives come before nouns. Second, they might spot that the words ending in *-st* come from other words (great→greatest, fine→finest) and that the *-st* ending is used to rank qualities in order of importance or intensity. These observations are not enough for them to learn the rule of superlative adjective formation in English, but it will give them a head start in understanding the rule when finally taught it in a grammar book or through specific exercises.

Traditionally, course books used to teach the rules first and then ask you to apply them. This method can be faster and it suits some students well. More up-to-date courses encourage students to work out why words change in different contexts and so deduce grammatical rules for themselves. Through actively engaging in this process, you are more likely to remember what you have learned and to use it more appropriately.

Functions

Recent theoretical work in linguistics has led to another classification of language based on 'functions', that is the purposes for which language is used. The underlying meaning of a grammatically simple sentence is not always obvious. The words 'close the door' can be a request to stop a draught or a warning that something confidential is about to be said. How you interpret a sentence depends on the circumstances and on the attitudes and relationship of the speakers. This is another reason why the cultural component of language is so important.

Functions are divided into categories such as 'making polite requests', 'asking for information', 'greeting people' and many more. Individual expressions used to carry out these functions are called 'function exponents'. So, for example, in English, 'Hallo, how are you?' is a function exponent of 'greeting people'. It's a good idea to organize these exponents in your dossier under headings such as 'stating obligation', 'likes and dislikes', 'disagreeing' and so on (see examples below).

STATING OBLIGATION

Saying what you can't do

no puedo
no tengo derecho
no es permitido

Saying what you must do

me hace falta
tengo que

LIKES AND DISLIKES

Talking about likes

das gefällt mir prima
das ist toll
ich möchte gern

Talking about dislikes

so geht es nicht
wie entsetzlich
einfach unmöglich

Classifying language by function has several advantages: above all, it enables you to know how vocabulary, grammar, intonation and even gesture are put together to achieve certain objectives. Function exponents are rarely literal translations and are often idiomatic constructions unique to a language. In fact, translating such expressions literally is to be avoided and may destroy the meaning.

Register

I don't care what your dictionary says — This is not the time for 'Standard French' Doris!

Another way of categorizing language is through register. In our native tongue most of us instinctively adapt our speech to the circumstances in which we find ourselves. In second-language learning, however, it's only relatively recently that teachers have emphasized the importance of using appropriate language, that is saying the right thing at the right time. Register is often divided into levels: from very relaxed speech, which can include slang (and even obscenities), through informal speech, used for instance among close friends, to a level which is usually called 'standard', that is polite and neutral, inoffensive and acceptable in all social groups. On the whole, this is the sort of language that you'll learn in most language course books or materials.

It is of course important to use the right register for the situation. Course materials and books are only just beginning to alert students to questions of register, so you should look out for appropriacy of usage when consulting your dictionary. An asterisk, for example, often denotes slang. You could also use your dossier to record different registers, following the guidance given in your course book or dictionary.

4   The four skills

Language learning involves four basic skills – listening, speaking, reading and writing. They may be used separately or, more often, in combination. Each of these major skills has its own sub-skills. For example, reading can be divided into reading aloud, skimming materials to understand the drift of a passage, scanning for specific information, and so on. Speaking and writing are known as **productive** skills because the student is required to originate the language. Reading and listening are known as **receptive** skills because the student absorbs and processes input. Most adult learners want to be able to listen and speak effectively because they wish to put their knowledge to practical use. To some extent, though, speaking and listening may be considered the two more difficult skills because they require the ability to react spontaneously and appropriately in new situations. However, all four skills are closely related and any improvement in listening and reading will help with the productive skills of speaking and writing.

ACTION
POINT
Which skill or combination of skills is most important to you? Which do you most need to practise and improve? Are there any particular tasks associated with these skills which you consider especially important? Record your responses in your dossier – this will help you prioritize your time and activities. Make regular checks on your progress in these key areas of learning.

Listening

Most modern course materials include audio cassettes or audio software. In fact, you really should not consider buying a foreign-language course unless it does come with recorded speech. There is no other way for you to link the printed word and its sound – unless you are lucky enough to have a teacher or good speaker of the language at hand.

If you ask students which skill they most wish to acquire, they usually say they want to be able to speak the foreign language fluently. Yet when language teachers are asked to prioritize, they often reply that knowing how to listen effectively is even more important. This is because students can be trained to look and sound convincing in a small number of well-defined situations, but can subsequently have great difficulty in understanding, and therefore in responding to, something which a native speaker has said.

So why should listening be considered such a complex skill to learn?

Think about why it can be so difficult to understand spoken foreign language. Look back at your record of progress on the various listening activities you have done. Try to identify what you find particularly difficult and note these points in your dossier.

How many of your ideas coincide with ours?

- **Speed of delivery** Many beginners in a foreign language comment on how fast native speakers talk. It is true that some languages are spoken faster than others. Peninsular Spanish is a good example. German, on the other hand, tends to be spoken more slowly than English. On the whole, French is spoken at about the same speed as English. What happens, of course, is that the beginner cannot yet discriminate between sounds or tell where one word ends and another begins. With practice, students begin to recognize and to differentiate between sounds. You will find that, after a month or two of practice, material which you listened to at the beginning of your course, and which may have seemed difficult at the outset, has become much more accessible.

- **Content** What native speakers say is not necessarily expressed in the way foreign learners expect. You may have worked on a situation ('in the bank', for instance) and feel confident with the expressions that occur in that context. But the bank clerk may say something quite different from what you expected. You will need to develop your speed of reaction so that you can respond appropriately.

THE BANK

- **Accents** English speakers have a variety of different accents, depending on where they come from. The same is true for speakers of other languages. As a foreign-language learner, you need to be able to handle a variety of voices and sounds in your chosen language.

The recordings which accompany your course book may contain authentic material – that is, real people speaking in their natural environment. You may find this difficult to cope with at first, but do persevere. The advantage of authentic over studio-recorded material is that you'll be learning, right from the start, to process your chosen language as you will hear it in the foreign country.

Listening strategies

- First of all – relax! You're not expected to understand everything immediately. It's a good idea to listen to a passage once all the way through and then to break it down into shorter sections for subsequent listening. You may find that the longer passages are already divided for you, but you will also need to listen to these sub-divisions in short, manageable chunks.

- Work from what you already know. The scene is usually set for you, either in the title or in a short introduction to the recorded passage. You can therefore assume that certain ground will be covered in that passage.

- Think about how the speakers sound. Are they angry, sad, quiet? What sort of age are they? Do you recognize any words which sound similar to English? If a transcript is provided, it will indicate any words or phrases which may look similar to English, but in fact sound quite different.

- Don't listen out for everything. Most course books ask you to answer questions or note specific information, so be selective. Leave extraneous material aside.

- If you do miss something, leave it and move on. If you are always a few seconds behind, you will miss what is coming up, as well as what has gone before. Authentic conversation is notoriously repetitive: you may find that points raised earlier crop up again, so you can have a second go.

- Listen again and again. The more you listen, the easier it will become. At the first listening, you may understand only one small point. By the sixth or seventh time, most information will be falling into place. Next day, play the recording again. You will find that not only do you still understand and remember yesterday's information, but one or two further points will now become clear.

ACTION POINT

Choose a recording and use it to try out the stategies outlined above. Identify which parts of the recording you find more difficult to understand and which are easier to follow. If possible, listen with someone who is of a similar level to you. You can share information and fit the jigsaw together, piece by piece.

Your course book may include transcripts of the recorded speech. A word of warning here. Try to resist reading them before you listen to the recording. The object with recorded materials is to sharpen your listening rather than your reading skills. As in music, so in language – it's a question of training the ear. You should, then, use any transcripts with discretion – perhaps for pronunciation or intonation practice. And remember, too, that conversations, because they are spontaneous, may contain errors made by the speakers. Your course materials will probably alert you to these errors, so that you don't take them as a model.

ACTION POINT

Record a conversation, in English, between friends – preferably without their knowing. Then play it back. You'll be surprised at how it sounds. Language does not move forward smoothly and logically from one point to the next. It backtracks, repeats, hesitates and lurches, and people make mistakes. Knowing that spoken language is not a prepared and highly polished speech can help you both to understand the foreign language and to feel more confident about speaking it.

Reading

When you first start to learn a foreign language, reading may not pose too much of a problem. Reading matter is carefully controlled and graded at the early stages and you have plenty of time to work out what it means. Later on, though, reading passages might contain a percentage of words (or constructions) that are unfamiliar and this can pose problems. Again, there are strategies which can help you through.

Reading strategies

- As with listening, put the information into context first. Look at any diagrams, pictures or photographs that accompany the text. Think about the title. Often the first and last sentences of a passage indicate its content, especially if it has been taken from the press. Use these clues to work out the gist of the passage and the general ideas the writer wants to convey.

- The previous point leads us to a strategy which should be general practice: that is, to work from the general to the particular, rather than vice versa. Many of us were taught to start with the opening sentence of a passage and then to work through the rest word by word. One false move and you found yourself on entirely the wrong track. It's much more effective to look at the passage first as a whole, then at sections, paragraphs, sentences, phrases and key words. Although this method might produce the occasional misinterpretation, it will lead to a good understanding of the general gist of the passage. The first part of this process (understanding the general drift) is called **skimming** or **gist comprehension**.

- Think about why you are reading the passage. You may be interested in a particular piece of information. For example, you may be asked to answer specific questions whose answers are to be found in one particular section of the text. In this case, you may not need to read the entire passage, but simply to pinpoint the relevant paragraph and work on that. Reading a passage for specific information is called **scanning**.

- Once you've reached the word level, ask yourself the following questions before consulting the dictionary. They may help you to guess the meaning of words you're unsure about.

  - Is the word a cognate, that is, does it resemble an English word? Many words in European languages have a common origin and therefore look much the same and have similar meanings. You can usually assume that these words are related, although they are unlikely to be exact equivalents. 'Mutton' and *mouton*, for instance, are not quite the same thing, and in Spanish *argumento* can mean 'plot' or 'story-line' rather than the English 'argument'.

  - Is there a pattern which can help with meaning? On the simplest level, French words ending in *-é* like *société* often end in *-y* in English. Spanish *-ando* and *-iendo* verbs endings are equivalent to the English *-ing*: *mirando*, looking. Italian *-azione* endings are the equivalent of *-ation* endings in English: *nazione,* nation; *conversazione,* conversation. There are many other patterns that you can work out for yourself as you progress through a language course. By knowing a few simple patterns you can significantly increase your vocabulary. You will find a lot of useful information about word formations in most modern dictionaries.

  - Can you work out whether the word you don't know is a verb, adjective, noun or preposition? If you can, it narrows your choice considerably and enables you to make an informed guess as to its meaning, taking into account the content of the rest of the passage.

Speaking

As noted earlier, most people want to speak the foreign language as well as possible, yet this is not always a very easy goal to achieve. It isn't hard to see why. Many different skills – pronunciation, intonation, control of vocabulary, manipulation of grammar – are being handled concurrently and at speed. Again, there are strategies which can put you on the road to both accuracy and fluency in oral skills.

Speaking strategies

- Some language is purely 'transactional' – that is, it involves communication between people for a particular purpose. Buying items in shops or purchasing train tickets falls into this category. You can prepare for these situations by learning the required phrases off by heart and practising them. Most foreign-language materials suggest activities such as role-plays to help you with this. However, you'll still have to cope with unexpected replies.

- You can, of course, guess the words that you don't know. The more you understand how the foreign language works, the more likely you are to create words which, even if they don't exist, could easily do so. They will be quite comprehensible to the native speaker and it's very likely that he or she will supply you afterwards with the correct variant.

- When you're talking to others in the foreign language, use them to 'feed' you the correct vocabulary and structures. Pick up what they say and bat the linguistic ball back, changing verb endings if you need to.

- Learn the foreign-language equivalents of phrases such as 'Sorry, I didn't understand' or 'Could you write that down for me?' These are useful in building up a store of coping strategies. They broaden your vocabulary and allow you to extricate yourself from potentially tricky situations.

- Do as much reading out loud as you can. This aids memorization of vocabulary and structures, as well as helping you to get your tongue round the language. Speaking other languages does not feel the same as speaking English because you use all sorts of different muscles around the mouth and throat. It is useful for you to become aware of those physical changes. Why not look into a mirror sometimes when you're practising? This will make you more aware of how your tongue and lips are moving.

This will make you more aware of how your tongue and lips are moving.

- Take every opportunity to speak. You could begin by repeating simple exercises or reading short dialogues or conversations from your course book. When you feel confident, try recording yourself. If you have two cassette recorders or appropriate computer facilities, you can listen to your recording and to the original at the same time. Compare your performance with that of the native speakers, note down any differences and try again. At a later stage, you could try delivering a short talk or lecture. Prepare brief notes about what you want to say, but don't read from them – use them as an *aide-memoire*, glancing at them from time to time to refresh your memory. Some people find index cards a good way of organizing what they want to say. You may dislike the idea of recording your own voice, especially when speaking a foreign language. Try to overcome this; no one else is listening to you and, if you don't listen to yourself, you have no idea about how you sound to others.

- Take specific phrases or sentences and practise speaking them out loud in different tones and at different pitches. The same phrase can be said harshly or softly, authoritatively or casually. The idea is to vary the way you say a phrase, but not what you say. In this way, you learn to concentrate on one sub-skill at a time rather than on many simultaneously.

- Think about pronunciation and intonation and how you can improve them. It is probably fair to say that adults learning another language are unlikely to acquire a perfect accent. However, you can go a long way to sounding convincing by concentrating on speed and intonation and by attending to detail such as stress (giving some syllables more emphasis than others). In English, for example, black **bird** is different in meaning from **black**bird.

ACTION POINT

Think about opportunities you can find for practising your speaking skills. These might include the following.

- Talking to another member of your family who is also learning the foreign language.

- Talking to native speakers who live near you.

- Talking to yourself, in the privacy of your own home or car, or to any captive audience (a pet, a house plant!). For example, you could think aloud in the foreign language, planning what you intend to do later in the day or mulling over what has already happened.

- Going to an evening class in the foreign language of your choice to get some oral practice, both with your teacher and with other students through role-play and pair work.

List these opportunities in your dossier and add to them as ideas occur to you.

Writing

There are two ways of looking at writing. First, there is the writing that you do as an aid to support your learning: making notes, writing down words to see if you can spell them correctly, and so on. Then there is the sort of writing which you do to create a meaning and to pass on a message to someone else.

Making notes to aid learning

We have already mentioned different learning styles. You may find that writing is one of the ways which helps you memorize structures or items of vocabulary. It is, after all, another sense that we are calling into play, in what we have described as a multi-sensory approach. The sheer physical act of putting pen to paper or fingers to keyboard can reinforce material which might escape us if simply heard or repeated out loud.

Think this through, however, before embarking on a programme of writing notes. There are some people who find the written word positively unhelpful for their pronunciation. Some languages – French and English are good examples – are not phonetic, that is, spelling does not reflect pronunciation. Think about whether seeing (or producing) the written word interferes with the way you speak. You may need to postpone writing until you feel confident about the way words are pronounced and how natural-sounding pronunciation in the foreign language is achieved.

If you do find that writing helps you memorize, try the following.

- Take notes while listening to the foreign language (on video, audio cassette, computer or on the radio) not as an activity in itself, but simply to help you continue listening without losing concentration.
- When you have finished studying a unit, chapter or section in your course book, write down the salient facts (or the things which were new to you).
- After listening to a recorded speech, write down a short summary of what you have heard.

Creative writing strategies

Writing in a foreign language is not easy. If, for instance, you're going to send a formal letter, your grammar, spelling and punctuation should be as correct as possible and you also need to use the right register.

Unless you're a business student or have chosen to buy a commercially oriented course book, you won't be learning to write a business letter or draw up a formal contract. However, there is no reason why you shouldn't be able to write a friendly message or a card, a brief letter asking for information, or a short report from notes made on a video or audio extract. You'll also find that writing is a useful by-product of other activities and that it is a good way of consolidating and extending other skills.

- Before you start to write, make two headings: 'ideas' and 'phrases'. Underneath them list what you are going to say and how you are going to say it. Don't worry at this stage about ordering your ideas. Just keep adding to the list as things occur to you. Don't rush this process. Take a day or two to mull over your ideas and to allow words and phrases which you have been reading or learning to come back to you.

- Decide on the register you wish to adopt. A letter to a friend will be informal and you'll need to use the appropriate form of address. On the other hand, a letter of complaint has to be formal. Make sure you don't switch from one tone to another within the same piece.

- When you do start to write, begin with the simple phrases and sentences you already know. Once you are happy with the basic structure, you can elaborate on it in the following ways.

  - See whether you can add a few adjectives. At the outset, these will be the most common ones, but you can use the notes in your dossier, your course materials or the dictionary to expand the range and variety of the language you use.

  - Try using link words to relate one sentence or short paragraph to the next. These will lead the reader on to the next point in a logical and pleasing way.

  - Make sure you have an introduction and conclusion, even if they are brief. You'll find that some of the more recently published dictionaries have supplements with ideas on how to begin and end letters, or on how to write reports and essays.

  - When you've finished, read what you have written out loud. The more you study your chosen foreign language, the more sensitive you will become to the language and things which begin to sound 'not quite right' can be removed or altered.

  - Check your grammar, punctuation and spelling. If you're not absolutely certain how a word is written, look it up. Check for agreements and tenses, tracing which words go with which, making sure that adjectives agree with their noun, that plural subjects have plural verbs, and so on. It is a good idea to carry out several checks, focusing on one aspect, such as the use of tenses, each time.

5   Learning vocabulary

This section deals with words – the building blocks of language. How do we learn them? Which ones should we learn?

Recently, more emphasis has been given to the learning of vocabulary. Students are keen to develop this area because, although you can go a long way on comparatively few words, there is no doubt that the more vocabulary you know, the easier it will be to express yourself. This gives rise to two questions.

- Which words and phrases should I learn?
- How should I learn them?

We will look at these areas in turn.

Which words and phrases should I learn?

It is not a good idea to learn all new words and phrases indiscriminately. The task would be huge. Before you start making lists, think about selecting which words are useful to you and give them special attention.

- Decide whether you need simply to recognize the new word or phrase you have just come across or whether you want to use it actively – that is, will you want to say it or write it yourself or do you wish just to understand it? 'Active' vocabulary will include everyday, informal areas or topics of personal interest. It will enable you to describe people, places and events and will include all the common verbs. You will need to learn these words well enough to be able to call them up at will and handle their different forms. Words that you have relegated to the 'recognition' category need only be recognized and understood in context.
- Think about which words are useful to you personally. If you collect ornamental fans as a hobby, you'll want to know the foreign-language equivalent. Although 'fan' is not a high-frequency word in itself, you will be using it a great deal if you are describing yourself and your leisure activities in your chosen foreign language.

How should I learn them?

We suggested earlier that there are many different ways of learning and that you need to think about your preferred learning style. There is no 'right' method. Discover what suits you the best and stick to it. Overleaf are some suggestions.

- Is your memory for things you hear better than your visual memory? In other words, do you learn more efficiently by listening than by seeing? If so, you could record new vocabulary items on cassette and play them when you have a spare moment.

- On the other hand, your visual memory may be more developed. You could try writing out new words on index cards and sorting through them at odd moments. Some learners write out new words on stickers and put them in strategic places – on the fridge or on the bathroom mirror for example.

- Do you respond to colour? We have already mentioned that some people record vocabulary items by colour coding them according to gender.

- Some language teaching methods advocate using both sides of the brain. The function of the left side of the brain is analytic, while that of the right is creative. You could activate both parts of the brain while learning vocabulary in the following way. Categorize new items according to some overall plan. It could be grammatical if you divide words into verbs, nouns or adjectives, or it could be vocabulary-based if you categorize them according to meaning. This takes care of the analysis. Then try to activate the right side of the brain. You could do this by illustrating each new word with a line drawing or, if you're not artistically inclined, by visualizing the item in your mind.

- Another trick is to associate the foreign word with another English word or perhaps with an idea – the more absurd the better. An example: a colleague trying to reactivate her French wanted to describe her office as a rabbit hutch. A French colleague told her that the word she wanted was *un clapier*. The word didn't seem to stick until she imagined herself crouching in a rabbit hutch and clapping for all she was worth! The word is now firmly embedded in her memory – along with the image of herself in the rabbit hutch.

'un clapier'

- Mind-maps are often used for fixing different items in the memory. Start off with a key word or phrase and then jot down items which are related to that word/phrase. The idea is that words are seen in relation to others, which is how they exist in reality. This is why it is not a good idea to try to memorize words out of context. Rather than learning vocabulary lists, always create a phrase or sentence for each word. This will help you remember not only the word itself, but how it is used. Below are two examples of mind-maps.

• You may already know about mnemonics – tricks to help you improve your memory. One well-known technique consists of isolating the first letter of a series of words which you want to remember and making up a sentence which includes those letters in order. Richard Of York Gave Battle In Vain is the classic way to remember the colours of the rainbow.

ACTION POINT   Try inventing your own mnemonics for language points that you're having difficulty remembering. Record these mnemonics in your dossier, on a separate page. If they're in the foreign language, that's a bonus.

6 Using video

You may never have thought about using video for learning a language. Indeed, the course materials you are working through may not include a video component. But quite a number of modern courses do have related videos and several language courses are available on television, where programmes can be recorded for study at a more convenient time. Even if you're not following a television-based course, you might find it interesting to record programmes broadcast in the language of your choice. News programmes are especially useful as major items usually relate to familiar topics.

ACTION POINT   Note down some of the advantages of using video to learn a foreign language.

Here are some of the advantages we would list.

- Understanding foreign speech is much easier if you can see the speaker or speakers in their real surroundings. And it is far more natural to see at the same time as hearing. This is how we have evolved over millions of years, and only a few modern inventions (radio, telephone, audio cassettes) separate sound from vision.

- Many people dislike using the telephone or language laboratories because the lack of vision is distracting or causes anxiety. They find the sight and sound combination far more comfortable.

- Video is an excellent resource which should be exploited to the full because it helps train visual memory.

- Video adds variety. Earlier, we discussed the importance of motivation, especially as language learning can be a lonely and repetitive business. An engaging shot of something interesting on video (with a commentary in the foreign language) can lift morale and provide the motivation to go on.

- Video is excellent for gist comprehension. As with reading texts, video can be viewed as a whole, rather than working on all the details. Try to enjoy the total visual experience.

- Video gives an insight into the way of life and culture of the people whose language you are studying. This would not be possible by using just text- or audio-based material. It is impossible to understand language without also understanding the way of life that underpins it.

- Some phrases and expressions cannot be understood without accompanying gestures, and video can demonstrate immediately what these are. Many languages (Italian, Spanish, Greek, Arabic are good examples) depend heavily on gesture – indeed, it is almost like a parallel language. It is interesting for foreign-language students to work out what these gestures mean and try to imitate some of the more common ones themselves.

What sort of exercises?

Throughout this guide we have emphasized that language learning must be dynamic. If your course includes video material, there will be a variety of different activities for you to complete. For instance, you might be asked to look out for certain objects in a video sequence or perhaps to match phrases from the text with phrases said by those appearing on screen. On other occasions, you might be asked to use video as a preparation for other exercises. Sometimes video is used as a 'lead-in', to provide the context in which you are going to work, in much the same way as the title or illustrations in a reading text might be used to introduce a topic.

If you're using language programmes from the television as your video material, try some of these ideas.

- Once you are familiar with a sequence, turn down the sound and provide your own commentary. You could play the role of a programme presenter, interviewer or character, depending on what sort of material you're studying. A sequence lasting a minute or two will be quite sufficient.

- If you can get hold of a transcript of the programme (by writing in for the Teachers' Notes, for instance, or buying the book which accompanies the series), you could try concentrating on one character only. Choose a short section and read it out loud as the character speaks. Try to read at the same speed. You'll need to do this several times.

- In the transcript you could blank out some of the key words from the section you've been working on. After a week or so, come back to the transcript and see if you can fill in the gaps. Check that you were right by playing the video sequence again.

Some practical advice

Now that you are using your video machine for study rather than just for pleasure, you need to become familiar with its operation.

- Make sure you use the remote rather than the manual control and that you know what all the buttons are for.

- Before you begin, adjust the set for brightness and colour.

- You may also need to adjust the volume and tone. Normally you need more treble and less bass for speech.

- Make sure that you're switched to the video channel; otherwise you'll find a TV channel breaking through when you pause for a while or stop your machine.

- You'll find that the pause button is not as sensitive as that on an audio cassette recorder. You'll probably have to rewind a little before beginning to replay. With practice you'll soon find out how much.

- Store the video upright in its case.

- Clean the video heads occasionally with a cleaning tape.

7   Using audio

Listening exercises

We have already mentioned the benefits of using authentic material to develop your listening skills, namely that in listening to native speakers right from the start you will begin to develop the skills necessary to handle speed of delivery, content and a range of accents and voices. Most audio materials provide a variety of listening exercises designed to help you understand what is being said: at times in order to get a general picture; at others to concentrate on something very specific.

Speaking exercises

You will be doing a lot of learning on your own and so you must take full advantage of the speaking exercises provided by any scripted audio material. In order to reproduce what you've heard, or to express something which is relevant to your own situation, you must first understand which words and phrases to use, how to pronounce them and how your voice should sound when you're speaking (intonation). Speaking exercises are designed to familiarize you with and give you practice in all of the above. They are likely to range from repetition of phrases to 'gapped' dialogues, that is, you supply the missing part of a conversation when prompted. There may be opportunities for you to deliver a short monologue. With all speaking exercises, it's important to do them a number of times. This will help you to learn the language they contain and to improve your overall speaking skills and pronunciation.

Tip: when rewinding or cueing a tape, if your cassette player doesn't have an autocue, you may find it helps to depress the play button and rewind/cue button together, because the sound you hear gives you an idea of where the gaps between extracts are.

Recording yourself

As you work through your course materials, you will probably be asked to complete exercises aimed at helping you practise and improve your speaking skills. After you have practised several times, we do urge you to record your responses on a blank cassette. Although, as we said earlier, most of us find listening to our own voices strange, especially when speaking in a foreign language, the long-term benefits of doing this are such that you should persevere. You will be able to play back your responses and judge them more objectively, paying particular attention to your pronunciation and intonation, perhaps even singling out the words or phrases you had difficulty with and concentrating on improving them. By doing this you should be able to notice how your speaking ability is improving as you work through the course.

General guidelines

It's difficult to give you precise instructions on how to record, as everything depends on the equipment you intend to use. Always refer to the instructions booklet of your machine(s) for advice. However, there are certain general rules that you should follow.

- **Never attempt to record directly on to a master tape** (i.e. one supplied as part of your course materials). If you do, you risk erasing what is on it.

- Do not record until you feel you are ready to do so.

- Do not record when you are in a rush: take your time, relax!

- Record somewhere where the level of background noise is low and at a time when you are unlikely to be interrupted.

- Experiment with how you position yourself in relation to the microphone in order to get the clearest recording. You shouldn't need to get too close or hunch yourself up in an uncomfortable position.

- Always listen to what you have done in order to judge your performance and, of course, to make sure that no technical hitch has stopped you recording at all!

Completing 'gapped' dialogues

When you are asked to complete a 'gapped' dialogue, you will normally find that sufficient space for your response has been left on the master tape. To record yourself, follow the procedures below.

- If you have a twin-deck machine, place the master tape in the playback section and your blank tape on which you will record your responses in the record section. (Make sure that this blank tape is wound on past the leader tape so you don't lose the beginning of what you want to record.) Once you feel ready, start the blank tape recording, press play for the master tape and concentrate on speaking.

- If you have a cassette player with a recording facility and microphone and another with a playback-only facility, it is perfectly possible to make good recordings, even without linking the machines with the appropriate leads.

Put the master tape in the machine with the playback-only facility and place this machine so that its speaker is near to the microphone of the other machine (30–40 cm should be close enough). Put the blank tape in the machine with the record facility. When you are ready, start the blank tape recording, press play for the master tape and concentrate on speaking.

Remember that the audio activities described here can be carried out in private. It is well worth persevering with them as they will improve your confidence to speak the language. They provide opportunities to rehearse for the real thing later on.

8   Using a dictionary

A dictionary is one of the most useful tools that a language student can have, but because so much information is packed into a dictionary it should be used with care. Knowing how to use a dictionary effectively is one of the skills that you should learn at the same time as you learn your foreign language.

Shopping around

If you already have a dictionary that was published relatively recently, you do not need to go out and buy another one. However, if you are thinking of buying one, you may find the following pointers helpful.

- You may want to buy a bilingual one (that is, with one half in English and the other half in the foreign language) to start with and a monolingual one (only the foreign language) later. Although monolingual dictionaries give you more information, they may be more confusing than helpful at the early stages and we recommend you use a bilingual one to start with. If you can, go to a book shop with a good language department and browse through the dictionaries they have on offer, for something at the price you wish to pay.

- Size and portability are important. Big dictionaries give a lot of information, but are difficult to carry around. Smaller dictionaries fit into handbags or back pockets, but are fiddly and inevitably omit a lot of useful material.

- Look to see whether your dictionary gives you a phonetic transcription of all entries. This helps you with the pronunciation of individual words and is especially important for languages which are not spelled as they are pronounced.

- Look for a dictionary with verb tables. It is always useful to be able to refer to a dictionary for basic grammatical information.

- Your dictionary should give you plenty of examples of usage. As we said earlier, words almost never appear alone; they tend to occur in a particular context which you need to be aware of.

- Check when the dictionary was published or last revised. Electronic publishing makes it easier for reference books to be updated and revised frequently, so that if your dictionary was last revised ten years ago it is certainly out of date. All languages change with time, and vocabulary reflects new developments in technology or society. You cannot learn modern French (or Spanish or Greek or whatever) with a twenty-year-old dictionary.

- You may prefer to use an electronic dictionary. Some are available relatively cheaply on a gadget the size of a pocket calculator.

What you should know

- Dictionary entries are made under 'headwords', which give you information about that particular word. Make sure that you know the abbreviations your dictionary uses for grammatical words like adjective, verb and so on. This will enable you to sift through and select meanings more efficiently. Different meanings are listed in order of frequency – that is, the most common usage appears first.

- Modern dictionaries give a lot of useful information on register. Do pay attention to words marked familiar, slang, vulgar, etc. with an abbreviation, asterisk or other sign.

- If you have found the English translation for a particular foreign word (or vice versa), it is always a good idea to look it up in the opposite half of the dictionary. This will give you more information and ensure that, out of several possibilities, you have chosen the correct one.

- For some languages, irregular verbs can be awkward to find in a dictionary. If you can't find the word you're looking for, it might be an irregular verb. Look it up in the verb tables for further help.

- It is a good idea to note down related words when looking up a particular item in the dictionary. If you are looking up a verb, for instance, note down as well any irregular forms given with the entry. This technique will increase your vocabulary enormously with very little extra effort. (Remember that it is a good idea to build up these 'word families'. You could record them in a 'Vocabulary' section in your dossier.)

- Finally, you may find it tedious to look up every word, so try guessing the meaning first from the context or form. Try all the possible techniques we've already suggested for intelligent guess-work. Consult your dictionary only when you have exhausted them all. One exception to this rule is gender. Not knowing if a word is masculine, feminine or neuter can cause confusion and has repercussions on other words in the same sentence: so, if in doubt, check.

9 Attending a language class

Whatever your preferred method of study or the course book/materials which you've embarked upon, it is a good idea to attend a class or to join a self-help group in your chosen language. Working with others improves the incentive to learn as well as providing opportunities to practise the language with friends or colleagues.

ACTION POINT

In your dossier, make a list of the advantages of working with others in your chosen foreign language.

These are some of the points we came up with.

• You will have access to other learners and possibly to a tutor who will be able to give you advice, extra language practice and moral support.

• You will have a regular focus for your work. Knowing that you have a commitment on a particular day for which you have to prepare should boost your motivation.

• You will have the opportunity to use your language spontaneously, or 'live', which you cannot do on your own.

Getting the most out of a class

If you decide to join a class or group, start looking around for one in good time. Friends and acquaintances may be able to recommend one that they have attended in the past. If not, local authorities publish information about their classes. Your local Education Department, local colleges and universities are also good sources of information about what is available.

• Whether you attend on a formal or informal basis, be positive! A teacher with twenty students in the class cannot please everyone all the time. Try to get as much out of each activity as possible by being active and co-operative.

• Be open-minded! When you join a group or a class, you may find that some approaches suit you better than others. Don't dismiss any of them out of hand until you've given them a try.

• Do any work that has been suggested and create activities that work for you.

- Do try to attend regularly if you possibly can. Working with other people is a good way to keep up your motivation and momentum.

- If you do have any ideas or suggestions that could improve the group, don't keep them to yourself. Share your ideas with others and in this way you will be contributing positively to your learning.

Modern methods

If you haven't learned a language for a long time, you may find that startling changes have taken place in modern language-teaching methodology. Many of these changes are based on the ideas which you have been reading about in this guide, so you should have a fair idea of why you should carry out certain activities. If you haven't, ask. Here are a few examples of the sorts of exercise in which you may be asked to participate.

Ice-breaking activities

At the first meeting of your group you may be asked to do a survey of group members. This is a good exercise to begin with, because it practises relatively easy language while giving you the opportunity to get to know other members of the class and your teacher. Activities like this 'break the ice' and help to promote a relaxed feeling within the group. You're more likely to complete the course if you feel comfortable with your fellow students and with the teacher.

Questionnaires and surveys

This type of activity helps you practise asking people questions (for example about their likes and dislikes) and gives you a chance to answer the same questions. It also provides you with the opportunity to identify fellow students who share your interests and perhaps to find out who lives close to you so that you can share transport or hold language practice sessions. It is also something you could organize for yourself if you wish.

Pair work

You may be asked to work with another person in the group, either to practise a dialogue or to act out a situation or role-play. The advantage of pair work is that you get much more oral practice than if the tutor asks questions of the group as a whole. You also have the opportunity to rehearse in front of one person rather than in front of the whole group.

Language games

Games are usually designed to practise a specific structure or function, while providing some light relief after a more taxing activity.

10 Putting your learning into practice

Here are some suggestions for further activities that you might find useful. Try them when you would like a few more light-hearted things to do.

- Go and see a foreign film or borrow one from your local video shop. Try not to look at the subtitles.

- Buy a foreign-language magazine or newspaper. You will be surprised at how much you can understand, especially if you have already read similar articles in the UK press.

- Find a native speaker and offer to buy a drink or a meal in exchange for some foreign-language practice. She/he might be interested in your giving English lessons in exchange. Notice boards in your local college or university are a good source of people looking for this sort of arrangement.

- Suggest to a friend doing a similar course of study that he/she studies the language with you.

- Try to speak the language with other members of the family who have studied it themselves.

- Tune into a foreign radio station and do the washing up while listening to the news or a light-hearted quiz.

- See if you can tune into the foreign-language channels on cable TV or satellite, if you have access to the right equipment. Watching advertisements over and over again is an excellent way of learning language.

- Have a look at what your local library has in the way of foreign-language materials or novels.

- Buy yourself a cassette or CD of songs and sing along with it.

11 Glossary

Words marked with an asterisk in the following definitions are themselves explained in the glossary.

Agree, agreement   When we say that a word agrees with another, we mean that its spelling (and perhaps its pronunciation) changes according to the word which comes just before or just after it: 'one child' but 'three children'. In European languages such as French, Spanish, Italian and German, there is a greater need to pay attention to agreement than in English, due to gender* as well as number. Learners of German also need to pay special attention to case*.

Argot   1 A relaxed way of speaking, used among people who know each other well, in circumstances where they are concerned not with social status but with reinforcing group identity. In this meaning, it is the same as slang*.
2 Special languages shared by groups of people with a profession or a social feature in common. There is a military argot, a bakers' argot, an argot used by people who work with computers, etc. See jargon*.

Article   In English, the definite article is 'the'. The indefinite article is 'a', 'an' or 'some'. In European languages, the articles change according to gender* and number as well as to the words which they precede.

Auxiliary, auxiliary verb   Words like 'be', 'will', 'has' or 'had', when they are used to make up the tenses of verbs. In 'I **have** seen it' the auxiliary is 'have': it helps to form the perfect tense* of 'to see'.

Case   Describes the relationship between subjects* and objects* in a sentence – who does what to whom, for example. Understanding the cases (*Fälle*) is particularly important when learning German, where there are four different ones. These are usually referred to by the Latin names, that is nominative, genitive, dative and accusative.

Clause   Part of a sentence, made up of at least a subject* and a verb. The last two words of 'He is the way he is!' are a clause. See main clause* and sub-clause*.

Cognate   Means 'born together'. Hence two cognates are two words which are historically derived from the same source, although they are now part of two different languages. Some cognates look very much alike (*république* and 'republic'); others less so (*pueblo*, 'people'; *Tochter*, 'daughter'; *bœuf*, 'beef').

Colloquial, colloquialism   A colloquial word is one which is used in everyday informal situations. Less relaxed than argot* or slang*, a colloquial word can be used with less fear of giving offence. In English 'it's a whole new ball game' may be thought of as colloquial, whereas 'the situation has changed totally' is not.

Comparative   An adjective that represents either an increase or decrease in degree, for example, 'larger', 'more important', 'smaller', 'less significant'. See superlative*.

Conditional   Form of the verb used in phrases describing a desired or imagined state of affairs. In English it is expressed by 'would': 'I **would** go to Italy if I had the money.'

Conjugate, conjugation   Changing the form of verbs according to whether they refer to actions taking place in the past, the present or the future, and according to who or what is doing the action.

Conjunction   Words like 'but', 'that', 'though' in English, and their equivalents in other languages. These words connect sentences or parts of sentences.

Definite article   See article*.

Demonstrative   A word with which you demonstrate or show what is being talked about: for example, in English, 'this', 'these', 'those', 'that one', 'these ones'; in French, *ce, cet, cette, ces*; in Spanish, *este, esta, estos, estas*; in German, *dieser, jener, mancher*, etc.

Direct object, direct object pronoun   See object*.

'Faux-amis' or false friends   A pair of words from different languages which look as though they should mean the same, but in fact mean different or even opposite things. In French *sensible* means 'sensitive' and in Spanish *tener constipado* means 'to have a head cold'.

Function of language, language function   The purpose for which language is used. If I say 'Aren't you cold?', my purpose may be to show concern for a fellow-being, or it may be to hint that I'm cold and that you should close the window.

Gender   In many languages nouns are either feminine or masculine (in some languages, German is an example, they can also be neuter). Some nouns have both a masculine and feminine form with different meanings. For example: in French, *une manœuvre* is 'a manoeuvre', but *un manœuvre* is 'a labourer'; in Spanish, *una guía* is 'a directory' or 'a street plan', while *un guía* is 'a male guide'; in German, *der Band* is 'the book' or 'the volume', *die Band* is 'the band' or 'the pop group' and *das Band* is 'the ribbon'. When talking about people, most feminine nouns apply to females, but by no means all (for example, a male victim in both French and Spanish is feminine). When referring to things and ideas, the division is even more arbitrary, so when you learn new nouns you have to memorize whether they are feminine, masculine or neuter.

Gist   The main meaning of a text or a conversation, regardless of details.

Idiomatic   An idiomatic phrase is made up of words that have a set meaning in everyday use that is different from the meaning of the separate words: 'a different kettle of fish' or 'a tall order'.

Imperative   Words used to give orders or instructions: for example 'do the dishes, please' or 'avoid sitting too long in front of the screen'.

Imperfect tense   Used to describe past events or states, particularly those that continued in the past, for example 'you **were** a very easy child', or were unfinished, for example 'he **was eating** his breakfast when the telephone rang'.

Impersonal verb   Verb whose action seems to be done by nobody or nothing in particular: for example, 'it's raining', in French *il pleut,* in Spanish *llueve,* and in German *es regnet.*

Indefinite article   See article*.

Indicative   A way of using a verb to state that something is or is not a fact or to ask whether something is a fact: for example, 'sets' in 'the sun sets in the west' and 'does … set' in 'does the sun set in the west?'

Indirect object, indirect object pronoun   See object*.

Infinitive   When you look them up in a dictionary, verbs are almost always listed in the infinitive: for example, 'to run', *courir* or *laufen.* The infinitive gives the idea of the action, event, process or state indicated by the verb, but doesn't say anything about who or what is performing the action, prompting the event, undergoing the process or experiencing the state, or about when it takes place.

Intonation   The rise and fall of the voice which expresses what the speaker is feeling: 'oh really?' can be said with the voice rising a little at the end (which shows slight surprise) or rising very markedly (which shows that the speaker is greatly surprised and doesn't quite believe what she/he is hearing).

Inversion   Reversing the order in which words are placed: 'was Peter aware of it?' is an example of verb–subject* inversion, compared with 'Peter was aware of it'.

Irregular verbs   Verbs which have an unpredictable pattern. Unlike regular verbs, whose form can be worked out easily once you know the basic pattern, irregular verbs have to be learned one by one.

Jargon   Words or expressions used (sometimes in a technical sense) by a particular group of people, which can make outsiders feel excluded. See argot 2*.

Liaison   Making a sound which runs two words together: for example, 'an apple' is pronounced a-n-apple.

Main clause   Central or essential part of a sentence which is qualified by sub-clauses* that may be adjectival or adverbial in function. See clause*.

Mood   The mood of a verb shows you whether what is being described is considered to be, for example, a fact, a command or a hypothesis. Moods corresponding to these ideas are called the indicative*, the imperative* and the subjunctive*.

Nasal sound, nasal vowel   In order for some vowel sounds to be pronounced correctly in languages such as French and Portuguese, air must go through the nasal passages. These sounds are known as nasal vowels and examples of them can be heard when pronouncing *vin, long* or *France.*

Object   The object of a verb is the person, thing or idea on which the action is carried out, or which receives the action. An object may be direct or indirect. It is direct when there is no preposition* in English between verb and object. 'Peter' is the direct object in 'I like Peter', but in 'I'll always listen to Julia' you have to put in 'to' between the verb 'listen' and its indirect object 'Julia'. When pronouns* are used instead of nouns, the same applies: 'him' is the direct object pronoun in 'I like him', and 'you' is the indirect object pronoun in 'I'll always listen to you'.

Participle   A past participle is a form of the verb used to make past tenses: they have **gone**, he has **read**, we have **decided**, *j'ai bu* (past participle of *boire*), *había bebido* (past participle of *beber*), *ich habe getrunken* (past participle of *trinken*). May also be used as an adjective: *il est ravi* (he is delighted), *ich bin verloren* (I am lost). The present participle shows simultaneous actions: *está durmiendo* (he is sleeping).

Passive   A form of the verb used when a person or thing has the action done to them, for example, 'then the food is chilled and shrink-wrapped' or 'he was listened to in silence by the audience'.

Perfect tense   In some modern European languages, a past tense used to describe events that took place and are now completed: *il a mangé des frites* (he ate some chips); *ha llegado de España* (he has arrived from Spain); *ich bin um acht Uhr angekommen* (I arrived at 8 o'clock).

Person   The person of a verb shows you who (or what) is doing the action. There are three 'persons' in the singular: first person – I; second person – you; third person – he/she/it. In the plural, the person of a verb is as follows: first person – we; second person – you; third person – they. In many European languages, verbs show the person by the form of the verb: for example, in Spanish, *hablo* (I speak), *hablas* (you speak); in French, *je pars* (I'm leaving), *il part* (he's leaving).

Pluperfect tense   A past tense showing that something happened in the past before another past event. For example, 'he **had eaten** before he went to the cinema'. In English, you recognize this form by the use of the auxiliary verb 'had'.

Possessive   A word showing to what or to whom something belongs. For example, in '**his** hand' 'his' is the possessive adjective; in 'it's not **yours**, it's **mine**!' 'yours' and 'mine' are possessive pronouns.

Prefix   Something added at the beginning of a word to give a particular meaning. For example, *super-* → supernatural, supersonic; *sub-* → subterranean, subway. See suffix*.

Preposition   A word that combines with a noun, pronoun* or noun equivalent to form a phrase linking the noun to the rest of the sentence. Examples of prepositions are 'to', 'at', 'under', 'by', 'of', 'from'.

Present tense   Tense used to describe a habitual action ('I read every day'), a single action in the present ('I open the door') or a continuous action in the present ('I am reading at the moment').

Pronoun   A word which is used to stand for a noun when you do not wish to repeat the noun (or, to rephrase this using a pronoun, 'when you do not wish to repeat **it**'). It acts as a substitute for a noun or phrase. See relative pronouns* and object*.

Reflexive verb   Often described as a verb showing an action which people do to themselves (for example, *se laver, lavarse, sich waschen*). Can also show actions which people do to each other (*s'embrasser, encontrarse, sich umarmen*) or which just happen (*s'évanouir*). Sometimes these verbs are called 'pronominal' because they always involve an extra pronoun* (yourself, myself, etc.).

Register   The style of language you use when relating to different people in different circumstances. There are many registers, on a scale from very formal (talking to a judge in court) to very relaxed or informal (talking among friends). See argot 1*, colloquial*, slang*.

Relative pronouns   Words like 'which', 'who', 'that'. They are used to relate parts of sentences to each other, for example 'the house **that** Jack built'.

Root   The part which a family of words has in common: **chemi**st, **chemi**stry, **chemi**cal. Also called a 'stem'*.

Scan   To read a text for specific information, by using appropriate reference points. For example, you would scan a railway timetable for an early morning train by running your eye along the line showing the 7 a.m. to 8 a.m. departures. You probably would not want to read the rest of the timetable.

Skim   To read a text by glancing through it to get the main ideas.

Slang   Very informal or jokey words used, for example, when talking to your friends. Not considered acceptable in some situations, for example at a job interview, but in others it can be appropriate to use slang for comic effect or to express strong emotions. See argot* and register*.

Stem   See root*.

Stress   The emphasis on a word or syllable. A language such as Spanish, which is phonetic, carries a symbol (´) to indicate where the stress falls in a word where this is unusual or irregular: *ilusión*.

Sub-clause   This is part of a sentence which cannot stand on its own. In German, a sub-clause is separated by the use of a comma; for example, *Der Tisch ist gedeckt, weil wir heute feiern wollen*. See clause* and main clause*.

Subject   The subject of the verb is the person or thing performing the action of the verb, or the person or thing being described by the verb: 'the boy stroked the dog' (subject: the boy); 'his thoughts were confused' (subject: his thoughts).

Subjunctive   A mood* of the verb which expresses doubt, uncertainty or hypothesis. Often the subjunctive form is used after certain phrases that denote these meanings: 'he may arrive in time', 'I suspect they may miss the train'.

Suffix   Something added to the end of a word to give a particular meaning. For example, *-let* is a suffix which adds the meaning 'little': 'pig' → 'piglet', 'book' → 'booklet'. See prefix*.

Superlative   A form expressing the idea of the most, the least: for example, 'the biggest' (*le plus grand*), 'the least quiet' (*el menos tranquilo*). See comparative*.